(713) 681-8300

TIM DUNCAN

Great Athletes

TIM DUNCAN

Jeremy Byman

MORGAN
REYNOLDS
Incorporated

Greensboro

TIM DUNCAN

Photo credits:AP/Worldwide Photos

Library of Congress Cataloging-in-Publication Data

Byman, Jeremy, 1944-
    Tim Duncan / Jeremy Byman.-- 1st ed.
        p. cm. -- (Great athletes)
    Includes bibliographical references (p.) and index.
    Summary: Discusses the life and career of the basketball superstar Tim Duncan, who was
drafted by the San Antonio Spurs in 1997.
    ISBN 1-883846-43-9 (lib. bdg.)
    1. Duncan, Tim, 1976---Juvenile literature. 2. Basketball players--United
States--Biography--Juvenile literature. [1. Duncan, Tim, 1976- 2. Basketball players.] I.
Title. II. Series.

GV884.D86 B96 2000
796.323'092--dc21
[B]

                                                                        00-035157

Printed in the United States of America
First Edition

To Maury Simon—
Sports fan extraordinaire

CONTENTS

Chapter One

It was the fifth game of the 1999 National Basketball Association championship series. The San Antonio Spurs, with its front line "Twin Towers" of David Robinson and Tim Duncan, had dominated the first 2 games of the best-of-seven series. Then the New York Knicks had come back behind the scrappy playing of Latrell Sprewell to win the third game. The Spurs won the fourth game through the solid play of Robinson and Duncan.

If the Spurs won the fifth game, the series was over. The San Antonio Spurs, the team that only two years before had one of the worst records in the NBA, would be the NBA Champions. David Robinson was one of the most solid and consistent players in the league, but the spark that had turned the Spurs into potential champions had been the team's acquisition of Tim Duncan.

The fifth game was played at the New York Knicks' home court—raucous Madison Square Garden. The exuberant Knicks fans would be sure to raise the roof rooting for the home team. The tension brewing under that roof came from one question: Would the Knicks be able to contain Tim Duncan and keep the series going, or would the Spurs superstar end the Knicks' hopes?

Both teams got off to a slow start. Near the end of the first quarter, thanks to Latrell Sprewell, the Knicks were leading 21-15, but Tim Duncan kept on his game. He made a baseline jump shot at the beginning of the second quarter that brought the Spurs to within one point. Then Tim sat out a few minutes to rest and the Knicks spurted to an eight-point lead. As the first half ended, Tim knew he would not sit out again.

The second half turned into a fierce duel between Tim and Latrell. Tim banked one off the glass for 2 points. Then Latrell gained control of the ball and spun away from the Spurs' defense to tie the score. Tim hit a hook shot; Latrell made a jump shot. Tim sent a jumper through the net from 18 feet, and Latrell charged the basket for a lay up. Latrell hit 14 straight points during one stretch. Tim scored 14 of San Antonio's 15 points.

With 3:12 to play in the fourth quarter, the Knicks were leading 77-75. Sprewell missed an easy shot. Tim sunk a foul shot, pulling the Spurs to within a point. With 47 seconds left, Spurs point guard Avery Johnson hit an 18-footer from the corner to give San Antonio a one-point lead. But 47 seconds is a lifetime in pro basketball. The Spurs knew that Latrell would make a move. With

2.1 seconds left in the game, Latrell raced through the lane and took a pass thrown from deep under the basket. He headed toward the basket for what looked like a sure goal.

With almost shocking speed, Tim stepped out to cover Latrell. Robinson also moved to block the shot. Suddenly, Sprewell found himself shadowed by the "Twin Towers." Sprewell took his shot, and it came up short.

The game was over. The San Antonio Spurs had won their first championship ever in a thrilling game, beating the Knicks 78-77. The jubilant players raced out onto the court to celebrate with their loved ones.

Tim Duncan was the undisputed hero of the series. In only his second year in the NBA, he had made all the important shots. Tim was named Most Valuable Player of the NBA Championship series. He had averaged 27.4 points and 14 rebounds a game. Knicks coach Jeff Van Gundy could only marvel: "Tim Duncan is obviously the best player in the NBA....Tim doesn't play like a second-year player. When you see a 7-footer hitting 20-foot bank shots, the guy's a special talent."

What is even more remarkable about Tim Duncan is the curious route he took to becoming the most dominant player in professional basketball.

Chapter Two

Unlike most NBA stars, Tim Duncan did not play competitive basketball until he was in high school. Few people played roundball where Tim grew up. The tiny island of St. Croix is one of the 3 Virgin Islands in the Caribbean off the southeast coast of the United States. St. Croix, an American territory, is a beautiful island of rain forests, a barrier reef, and tall mountains.

Timothy Theodore Duncan was the youngest of William and Ione Duncan's three children. William Duncan had many different jobs over the years. He has worked for an oil refinery, operated a hotel, and worked as a mason.

When Tim was born on April 25, 1976, Ione Duncan was thrilled to have a son. She already had two daughters. Ione was a hard-working mother and midwife, a person who assists during childbirth. She kept her children busy at school and at sports. "She pushed Tim hard," says Tim's brother-in-law, Ricky Lowery.

"She was a strong woman who made Tim work hard at what he did."

Ione started Tim and his sisters as competitive swimmers. She drove them back and forth to meets and volunteered as a timer. She was so determined to see her kids compete that she worked late at night so she could attend their swim meets during the day.

Sitting near the starting blocks, Ione whispered advice to Tim during his meets. Even from the other end of the pool, with his head underwater, he could hear her cheering. "She was my biggest fan," Tim said. "Every meet she was the loudest parent there. Somehow I could always pick out her voice yelling over everybody else." Ione would become so nervous for him during events that Tim had to remind her he was trying to concentrate on the race. Tim has never forgotten her motto: "Good, better, best. Never let it rest, Until your good is better, And your better's best."

Ione's determination paid off. All three Duncan children became successful young athletes. Cheryl, Tim's older sister, was a strong swimmer. Tim and his sister Tricia earned world rankings. Tricia brought honors to her home and family when she swam in the 1988 Olympics in Seoul, South Korea. She represented the Virgin Islands in the 100- and 200-meter backstroke. When he was only 13 years old, Tim was nationally ranked in the 400-meter freestyle. His records in the 50- and 100-meter freestyle still stand in St. Croix.

As his sisters grew older, they began to find new interests. Cheryl married and she and her husband, Ricky, moved to Ohio. Tricia began pursuing her career. Meanwhile, Tim skipped a grade in school and continued to work hard at swimming.

For Christmas of 1988, Cheryl and Ricky sent Tim a basketball goal. After William set up the goal for him, Tim shot some baskets, but he was more interested in hanging out with his friends and listening to music. Besides, who could he play with? Basketball was not a popular sport on St. Croix.

Then tragedy struck in Tim's life. In the summer of 1989, Ione discovered she had breast cancer. It was a shock for everyone. Although she had to undergo chemotherapy, she continued to work delivering babies.

Just as the family had begun to adjust to Ione's illness, a new tragedy struck. On September 17, 1989, St. Croix was hit by the massive hurricane Hugo. Fishing boats were tossed from the harbor into the downtown section of the capital city, Christiansted. Streets were blocked for months. Houses were destroyed, and schools were closed. The pool where Tim trained—the only one big enough for swim training on the island—was destroyed.

Even worse, the hospital where Ione worked and received chemotherapy treatments was severely damaged and lost power for days. She was unable to receive any treatment during this time.

Tim tried to continue training in the ocean after the pool was destroyed, but it was difficult. The waves threw his movements off and there was always the threat of sharks. He found he could not train as successfully as he had in the pool.

Then on April 24, 1990, Ione died. It was the day before Tim's fourteenth birthday. Tim had lost his mother and his biggest fan. After her death, he no longer wanted to swim.

Cheryl and Ricky moved back to St. Croix to help with the family. Ricky had played guard on a basketball team at a small college in Ohio. He began to teach Tim the fundamentals of the game on the goal they had sent him for Christmas. Ricky and Tim played one-on-one for hours everyday. Tim was already over 6' tall in the ninth grade. "I noticed he had talent," said Ricky. "Obviously, he had long arms and long hands. He was uncoordinated. But he had amazing hand-eye coordination. When he saw a shot go up, he knew exactly where it was going to come down."

Ricky started Tim at guard, and concentrated on teaching him to shoot from the perimeter. He showed his young brother-in-law how to use his body, how to move his feet, how to dribble. "I remember he would jump up with the ball sometimes and hit the bottom of the rim going up," said Ricky. "And then people would laugh at him." Tim just worked harder. Practicing with anyone wasn't easy. There were only four indoor basketball courts on the entire island of St. Croix, and they were usually reserved for volleyball! But Tim had found a new sport. "That's when I started playing basketball," he would say later.

When Tim joined his high school team, St. Dunstan's Episcopal, he started to develop as a good player. As a freshman guard, he stood 6' 1". After he grew nearly 8 inches in 3 years, he switched to center. "I played facing the basket. I would shoot threes and drive and dish. I wasn't anything close to being a real center." He worked on learning how to play with his back to the basket. He also began to be featured in stories published in the local newspaper. Although Tim's school did not keep records on basketball games, his high school coach remembers Tim once scored 40 points in a game and blocked 12 shots in another game.

The summer he was 15 years old, Tim went with Ricky to the Ohio State basketball camp. He spent a week playing against college players. Tim was able to hold his own in the rough and tumble, and he knew when he returned home that basketball was his sport.

As Tim approached his senior year, recruiters—the people who encourage star high school athletes to sign up with their college—began to take an interest in him. He did not attract as much attention as he would have if he lived in the United States. The

Virgin Islands are off the beaten track for television and newspaper reporters, and Tim had only been playing competitive basketball a few years. Few colleges had ever heard of him. Offers trickled in from Georgetown University in Washington D.C. and from the University of Delaware. Providence College offered him an athletic scholarship that would cover his tuition, room, and board. Then, in one of the great recruiting mistakes in college basketball history, Providence College decided to give the scholarship to another player. They asked Tim to come to the school as a walk-on, which meant he would not have a scholarship.

Dave Odom, the coach at Wake Forest University in Winston-Salem, North Carolina, had a better plan. Odom knew about Tim because a former Wake Forest player had visited St. Croix with a tour of NBA rookies. He had seen the 16-year-old hold his own against rising star Alonzo Mourning.

After Odom heard about Tim, he visited the Duncans in St. Croix in the summer of 1992, before Tim's senior year. Odom discovered that Tim was so shy he would rather watch television than look at him. The coach eventually sat down next to the set so that Tim could not avoid looking at him.

Odom grew a little impatient. He was sure Tim hadn't been listening to him explain what a good idea it would be for Tim to play for the Demon Deacons. He asked if he could turn off the television.

"In response to that he repeated back to me word for word what I had been telling him," Odom says. "I was amazed. He has this innate ability to look distracted but to take in everything around him." Modestly, Tim explained: "I was listening, but the 49ers were on. It was the fourth quarter."

Coach Odom should not have worried. His message had gotten through. Tim signed to play and study at Wake Forest. The boy who had only been playing basketball for 4 years was on his way to compete in the Atlantic Coast Conference, the toughest college basketball conference in the country.

Chapter Three

Because Tim had skipped a grade in elementary school, he was only 17 when he arrived on the Wake Forest campus in the summer of 1993. The other players on the Demon Deacons team knew Coach Odom might be taking a chance with him. "When Timmy came here, I heard stories from our coaches that he was a project," his teammate Randolph Childress remembers. "So one day I walk into the gym and see this tall guy who grabs a rebound, puts the ball between his legs, dribbles coast to coast and slams. I went to see our coaches, and I told them, 'Hey, there's a tall kid in the gym doing some incredible things, and if he's not Tim Duncan you better recruit him fast.'"

The 6'10" kid from the Virgin Islands fascinated other students on campus. They knew little about life on St. Croix. "Do you wear clothes down there?" one girl inquired. "No," replied Tim calmly. "I bought everything when I got here." He never told her that he was joking.

Tim also had a few things to learn about the United States. Randolph Childress claims (and Tim denies) the following conversation took place during his first semester at Wake:

"Where are you from?" Tim asked.

"D. C.," Childress replied.

"Where's that?"

"Washington, D. C."

"Where's that?"

"It's the nation's capital, for crissakes. It's where the president lives."

Coach Odom could see that Tim had enormous promise, but he planned to keep him on the bench most of the year so he could learn about the big-time college game. Then another new player, Makhtar Ndiaye of Senegal, was declared ineligible. Coach Odom had no choice. Tim took over at center.

At first, Tim was weak on defense, but he worked hard and quickly began to become a skilled shot blocker and rebounder. He also had to work on his passing game. In St. Croix, he had usually gone to the basket himself. In the Atlantic Coast Conference, or ACC, it was important to make strong assists as well as put up a lot of points.

Tim struggled in the beginning. His first college game was against the University of Alaska in Anchorage. He did not attempt a shot the entire game, and his team lost a heartbreaker, 70-68. The one good thing about the trip was that the boy from the tropics got to see snow for the first time.

In his second game, Tim finally started taking shots. In his first home game, against Winthrop College, Tim blocked 8 shots and scored 12 points. He was becoming a strong addition to the Deacons starting line-up.

Randolph Childress was the star of the Deacon team. He scored the points and snagged the headlines. In the beginning, Tim was mentioned near the end of the newspaper articles about their games—if he was mentioned at all.

Randolph was garnering career highs in point scoring, but Tim's contributions were edging into the double digits. The big victory in the early part of the season came when Wake edged number-one ranked Duke by a score of 69-68. This moved them to the top of the ACC.

In a win over Georgia Tech, Tim had 18 points and 16 rebounds. He took 14 points in the first half alone. It was a milestone game for Tim, but his teammate Randolph could not find the basket. In a loss against Virginia, Tim played hard defense, blocking shots left and right. After victories over North Carolina State and Rhode Island, the ACC named Tim Rookie of the Week. Only 3 weeks after becoming ACC Rookie of the Week he was named ACC Player of the Week

Things did not always go so smoothly. During a game against Clemson (80-69) Tim fouled out for the first time in his college career. Sharone Wright, Clemson's star center, had embarrassed him. "Sharone handed Tim his head," Odom remembers. "It was a man against a young boy, one thunder dunk after another. I got worried about Timmy. I called him into my office the next day and I eased my way into the conversation because I didn't want to scare him. Suddenly he interrupts me and says, 'Coach, I'm fine. I'm just out there having a good time.'"

The reporters had now taken notice of Tim. They were talking about his "huge impact" on the Wake team, giving it the "inside game" it had long lacked. Tim enjoyed the praise.

Tim entered the ACC tournament—the climax of the season—sixth in the conference in blocked shots and third in rebounds. In March, he was named to the all-ACC freshman team and came in second in the voting for Rookie of the Year.

Wake routed Georgia Tech 74-49 in their first game, but they were eliminated by Carolina 86-84 in the second game.

Even with the loss in the ACC tournament, the season was not over. Wake's win-loss record during the regular season had earned it a berth in the NCAA tournament for the fourth straight time. Tim was still learning important lessons. In a 68-58 victory over the College of Charleston, Tim played his best game of the year, with 16 points, 13 rebounds, and 8 blocks, but he was benched briefly in the second half for not being aggressive enough. "He got beat down the floor a couple of times, so I pulled him. I got on him pretty good. I told him when he was ready to play to let me know," said Coach Odom. "A few minutes later I felt a tug on my coat." Tim had learned his lesson. In the next 8 minutes, he had 10 points, 6 rebounds, and 4 blocks.

Wake was defeated in the second game of the tournament. It was an unsatisfying end to Tim's first college basketball season, but the basketball world had been put on notice. Tim Duncan had quickly established himself as one of the greatest freshman players in Wake Forest history. In his first 51 games, he set the school record for blocked shots with 124—the third most by a freshman at any college in the country. His total was more than those of NBA stars Shaquille O'Neal (115) and Marcus Camby (105) when they were college freshmen.

In the summer of 1994, Tim played for USA Basketball's Junior Team in Argentina and at the Goodwill Games in Moscow, where the team won the bronze medal. Later, he traveled with an ACC all-star team headed by Coach Odom that toured Brazil for 8 games. "Playing international ball has really helped my development," Tim said. "It gives me a chance to play against older, stronger, more experienced players."

Chapter Four

At the start of his sophomore season in 1994, Tim was a much-improved player. He controlled the perimeter around the basket as well as players who had been playing the game since childhood. The way he moved his body and the way he got in position around the basket convinced Coach Odom that Tim was the most naturally gifted big man he had ever seen play the game.

Wake had Childress back for another season and had added Ricky Peral at forward. The young team started the season ranked only fifth in the ACC, and Tim wanted to prove that this was too low.

Tim was now a favorite of newspaper reporters. He was interviewed before and after most games. Modest as always, he told them he had improved over his first season because of Randolph Childress, the star senior guard who was his best friend on the team. "He pushed me. He demands the best from you, just like he demands it of himself.... Now, I push along with him."

Tim's family followed his college career closely. His sister Tricia, who was working as a physical therapy aide in Baltimore, Maryland, attended many of the Wake games. Tricia would get so excited during the a game that she would scream whenever Tim's name was mentioned—even when he was called for a foul. She reminded Tim of their mother at his swim meets. Back home on St. Croix, his father would gather around the TV with his friends whenever ESPN carried the Wake Forest games. If he could not watch a game, he would read about it in the paper the next day. Thinking of Ione, Cheryl said, "Mom never got to see Timmy play ball seriously. But I think she's looking down from heaven cheering him on—the loudest voice among all the angels."

The 1994-95 season didn't start well for Wake Forest. The team barely squeezed out some victories and lost others because Tim and 6' 10" teammate Ricky Peral were being double-teamed. Finally, during a mid-December win over the College of Charleston, Tim broke free and scored a career-high 23 points and blocked 7 shots. A few nights later, he scored 24 points against the Citadel, gathering 15 rebounds and 5 blocked shots—all career highs. Tim was named ACC Player of the Week. He was now shooting a remarkable 75% from the field, and he led the league in shooting percentage, rebounds, and blocks.

A 74-64 victory over perennial basketball power Duke convinced Coach Odom that his team was going to be a major contender in the ACC. Duke tried to triple-team Randolph, now nicknamed "Mr. Outside," until he learned to evade them. Meanwhile Tim—"Mr. Inside"—blocked 7 shots, scored 18 points, and pulled down 8 rebounds against the taller and more physical Duke team.

Tim still had a few things to learn. When Wake lost 62-61 to top-ranked North Carolina, the Tarheels caught Tim off balance. They forced a penalty with 5 seconds left in the half. The Tarheels then took possession when Tim failed to get the ball in-bounds or to call for a time-out. "Randolph was open and I didn't get it to him," said an embarrassed Tim after the game. "I knew we had the time-out left. I was too late calling it." Aside from that one critical mistake, Tim had had a strong game. He blocked 7 Tarheel shots, scored 18 points, and grabbed 17 rebounds in a head-to-head contest against UNC star center Rasheed Wallace. He was more careful than other players, committing only 2.5 fouls a game. Coach Odom was proud of Tim's dedication, too. "He always looks at tape and studies the game," Odom said.

Tim was being described as one of the ACC's "super sophomore centers." His technique was now usually flawless. He could block a shot and keep the ball in bounds. When he took down a rebound he was totally in control of the ball. He was so dominant in controlling the game that he did not have to score big numbers to be a valuable part of the Wake Forest team, but he usually scored in the double digits.

In one mid-season assessment, Tim was ranked fourth in the nation. Tim's superb play attracted the attention of the NBA as it prepared for its June draft. Everyone wondered, would Tim join the NBA, or would he stay at Wake?

It was a critical year for turning professional. The next year a proposed salary cap would probably go into effect. This cap meant that rookies who signed up after the June draft would be paid millions of dollars *less* than those signing during that season.

Coach Odom knew all about the pressures on 19-year-old Tim. Agents focused on students who came from poor families. "They get to a kid and ask him or his family, 'Wouldn't you like to be rich?' Of course they would. They plant the feeling in the kid's head that he's got to support his family. They tell him he can be a millionaire and doesn't have to take Spanish or biology to do it. They find a weakness in the kid's make-up and play on that." Odom thought that the players should finish their education.

Tim refused to enter the NBA draft. He rejected the overtures from the agents. "To be honest, I'm not looking too far ahead," he said. "I mean, I've thought about the pros, obviously, but not to the extent that it would happen this year." He wanted to continue working on his game and to do well in his course work.

Tim told the agents of his decision early so he could concentrate on perfecting Coach Odom's game strategies. In a 64-52 victory over Clemson, Wake Forest trapped the Tigers in a "spider-web" zone defense. They played "loose," luring Clemson into the perimeter and closing in behind them. That way Clemson offense was forced to play one-on-one with Tim, who blocked or altered most of their shooting.

By the end of the regular season, Tim was averaging 16.5 points, 12.3 rebounds, 4.1 blocks per game. His field goal percentage was 58.4.

Wake Forest's successful season gained them a share of the regular-season basketball championship and the top seeding in the ACC Tournament. In the opening game against Virginia, Wake won 77-68. Tim scored 20 points and pumped up the whole team with his energetic play and his sizzling rebounding and blocking. His talent at drawing fouls knocked key Virginia players out of the game. Tim's dad had come up from St. Croix to see Tim play college basketball live for the first time. He enjoyed both the game and the snow that was falling outside.

The Deacons made it to the ACC championship game. They were matched against their nemesis, the University of North

Carolina. During the game, Tim picked up 3 fouls and the Deacons fell behind 38-33 at halftime. But they didn't panic. Odom talked Tim into being more careful and he managed to avoid any more fouls. He scored 16 points and snared 20 rebounds.

Randolph Childress was the real hero of this game. The rest of the team, fired by Randolph's superb shooting, rallied when they were down. During every time-out, Childress begged them to play harder. The two teams were tied 73-73 at the end of regulation. In overtime Randolph was inspiring, and his hot shooting finally won the game for them, 82-80. Wake Forest had finished the season with a 24-5 record, the best in 68 years.

Tim, who led the ACC in blocked shots with 135, was voted to the All-America third team. The National Association of Basketball Coaches named him the defensive player of the year. In the NCAA tournament, Wake cruised to victory over a much smaller North Carolina A&T team, then barely eked out a 64-59 second-round victory over Saint Louis University. Tim scored 25 points—almost half the team's points—and Randolph added 21 points. On one critical play, Tim realized that Wake's players were out of place, and a Saint Louis player had a clear shot from only 10 feet out. Tim raced over, blocked the shot backhanded, then hit it away for a fast break. Coach Odom called Tim's block "the biggest play in the game."

The Cinderella ride ended in the regional semifinals when Wake lost to Oklahoma State, 71-66. Tim had another great game, scoring a game-high 22 points. He won a duel against OSU's huge, All-America center, Bryant Reeves, but the rest of the Deacon team was not able to put the ball through the hoop. It had been a great season.

After the NCAA tournament ended, Tim signed up for summer school. Recalling his promise to his mother that he would get his college degree, he said, "I hope the talk of me possibly turning pro stops now." He had made it clear that he intended to continue his education.

Instead of worrying about the draft, Tim played basketball. As agents scratched their heads over his reluctance to go for the big money, Tim flew off to Japan with an American team and played in the World University Games. In the Japanese city of Fukuoka, he scored 21 points and helped the U.S. beat Japan 141-81 in the men's basketball final.

Chapter Five

By the summer of 1995, it was clear that Tim Duncan had come a long way from that 14-year-old kid who would rather hang out with his friends than play basketball. He spent the hot months working on all aspects of his game—passing, shooting, blocking, and ball handling. He readily admitted that he still had a great deal to learn. He knew that he had to continue to improve his game.

Tim was also motivated to improve because he would have an even larger burden on his shoulders during the 1995-96 season. Randolph Childress had graduated. Two sophomores now filled the backcourt duties—Jerry Braswell and Tony Rutland. Tim would have to be the team leader. His game would have to become more instinctual because he would need to focus more of his attention on what the other players were doing at all times.

At the beginning of his third season, Tim was named to the Associated Press' preseason All-America team. He was also the only one of the ACC's 1994-95 4 sophomore stars to return to college basketball for the new season. The others, including Rasheed Wallace of North Carolina—who Tim had dominated the season before—had decided to join the NBA. The lure of huge contracts and signing bonuses had been too strong for them to resist.

Tim's sense of humor made him popular with his teammates. They called him "Merlin," after King Arthur's magician, because he had a picture of Merlin dribbling a basketball tattooed on his chest. When they finished playing or studying, Tim and his teammates would go to professional wrestling matches or play paint ball games. Tim liked to pull practical jokes. One of his favorites was to pick his friends' pockets when they were not looking.

Wake faced Oklahoma State in the first game of the season, the team that had knocked them out of the NCAA tournament the previous year. Wake got revenge, winning 69-53. Tim scored 22 points and pulled down 17 rebounds. Several NBA scouts watched Tim ice the game with 9 baskets in a row after OSU came within 6 points of the Deacons. "I told our guys not to take a shot within 10 feet, because if they did, Duncan would make a 'WILSON' [the sporting goods maker's name stenciled on the side of the ball] imprint on their forehead," the Oklahoma State coach said.

In a match-up against second-ranked University of Massachusetts, though, Tim was bested by All-American center Marcus Camby. Camby was lightning-quick, and he had an excellent game with his back to the basket. In UMass' 60-46 win, Camby scored 17 points and pulled down 9 rebounds, but more importantly, he limited Tim to 9 points.

Wake Forest was playing a difficult schedule. Six of their non-conference games were against teams that had played in the previous season's NCAA Tournament. For the first time, now that Childress was gone, Tim was facing double- and triple-teaming in almost every game. It began to wear down his morale. During a game with Utah, Coach Odom decided to give him a pep talk at halftime. It worked. Tim scored 10 of his game-high 24 points in the final 5 minutes, and Wake won. That night, 21 NBA scouts eyed Tim from the stands.

When the Deacons met the Duke Blue Devils, Tim began to discover some of the other pressures that could come from being the center of attention. Halfway through the game the Duke fans started chanting "O-ver-rat-ed."

But the Duke fans had made a serious mistake. Until they started teasing him, Tim had scored just 14 points and produced more turnovers than field goals—partly because Duke was double-teaming him, but their ugly taunts fired him up. With less than 48 seconds to play, Duke led 54-53. Tim got the ball 15 feet from the basket. He dribbled backward against Duke center Greg Newton. Then he faked Newton out with a move toward the top of the lane, spun the other way and slammed home a shot that silenced the crowd and gave Wake a 55-54 lead. On the next Wake play, he again faked Newton with exactly the same move. Wake won 57-54, with Tim scoring 12 of the Deacons' last 16 points. It was the eighth-ranked Deacons' twelfth straight victory against ACC opponents.

With all of the time he was putting into basketball, Tim managed to keep up with his schoolwork. He studied French, World Civilizations, and courses for his Psychology major. He maintained a 2.7 grade-point average. Tim and Coach Odom both thought he could raise his average a full point if he did not spend so much time playing and practicing basketball.

Tim continued to learn how to break out of double-and triple-teaming. In a 77-64 victory over Maryland he scored and blocked shots at will and passed the ball to his undefended teammates for several assists. Everybody scored well, and Tim finished with his first career triple double, collecting 14 points, 15 rebounds, and a school-record 10 blocked shots.

Wake finally lost a conference game to hard charging Clemson, 55-41. It was their lowest offensive output in 16 years.

They had been the league's best three-point shooting team but in this game they missed 20 tries. Tim scored 20 points and grabbed 13 rebounds, but with most of the Clemson team in his face, he had just got off one shot during the first half.

As the season drew toward a close, NBA scouts, recruiters, and reporters again wondered if Tim would leave school early to join the NBA. Tim had not forgotten his promise to his mother to finish his education. There was also the chance that if he stayed he might be able to play for a team that went all the way to the NCAA championship. His game still needed work, especially his jump hook and his spin move. Coach Odom wanted him to use his strength more, power the ball to the basket, and rely less on his arms and his height.

Coach Odom was also quick to praise Tim for the improvements he had made. He worked with the two sophomore guards on the team to control the perimeter. His "vision," or ability to keep an eye on everything happening on the court, and to respond lightning fast to changes, made the difference is several close games. That basic shot for big men, the turnaround jumper, had improved. He also had a reliable hook shot. Tim was emerging as a good play-maker and was the smartest center in college basketball.

It is remarkable that Tim still wanted to improve his game

before moving to the pros. Many players with lesser ability had made the move to the big league, but from his days as a swimmer, Tim had always gone at his sports with a strong and steady determination to be better. His approach to basketball was the same. He simply was not going to be rushed before he thought it was time. And besides, he had promised his mother that he would earn a college degree.

To be certain, Tim still had some humbling moments on the court in college basketball. In Virginia's upset of Wake 67-49, Tim missed 14 of his 20 shots. Virginia muscled Tim, making it hard for him to shoot. Said one Virginia player, "He was getting frustrated. Tim on the court usually has a quiet demeanor, but after he missed some shots in the first half he went off. He was yelling at his teammates, 'I'm tired of this, get me the ball!' I was shocked."

The Deacons finished second in the ACC regular season. Tim was a unanimous pick to the Associated Press All-ACC team. He led the conference with 17 double doubles, including 9 in his last 13 games. He was approaching his third straight season of 100 or more blocked shots. Despite constant harassment, frequent fouls, and double- or triple-teams against him, Tim's averages per game were the most impressive in the league. He averaged 11.5 rebounds, 3.8 blocks, and finished second in scoring with 19.2, and his field goal percentage was 55.5. Wake had won 12 games and lost 4 in the ACC, while winning 20 against all opponents and losing only 5.

In the semifinal game of the ACC tournament, Wake beat Clemson 68-60 because Coach Odom took a chance by leaving Tim in despite foul trouble. Tim managed to avoid a fifth foul while scoring a game-high 22 points and pulling down a season-high 19 rebounds. Tim hit an amazing off-balance turnaround jumper from 17 feet. It bounced high off the front rim, banged the back rim, then dropped through. He finished Clemson off in the final 20 seconds with 3 free throws.

Between tournament games, Tim sat in the players' lounge, taking on any challengers in Mortal Kombat. "He kills everybody," teammate Rusty LaRue said. "He's a video-game god."

Wake beat Georgia Tech by one point in a thrilling 75-74 game for the ACC Tournament championship. Again, a fired-up Tim saved the day. Wake guard Tony Rutland went down with a sprained knee. Tim jumped and blocked the rim from Tech's Stephon Marbury, forcing him to miss a critical shot. Tim was named the event's Most Valuable Player after he scored 27 points and grabbed a tournament-final record 22.

It had been a joy to Tim that his father, William, and his sister Cheryl had watched the game from a seat not far from the Wake Forest bench. Said Tim, "It's great to be able to look into the

crowd and see someone you know and love and grew up with."
After the Deacons won the ACC Tournament, Tim was named the
ACC Player of the Year, and was elected to the NCAA All-
America first team. He averaged 19.6 points and 12.3 rebounds
during the series. He led in rebounds and blocks, was second in
field-goal percentage and scoring. He was a unanimous pick for
tournament MVP.

Reaching the NCAA semi-finals was the furthest Wake had
gone in the national tournament during Coach Odom's seven-year
career, but in the Midwest regional semifinal, Wake barely beat
Louisville 60-59. With Wake trailing 59-57, Tim found himself
one-on-one with Louisville center Samaki Walker. Tim dribbled,
drop-stepped toward the basket, and hit a bank shot. When he
was fouled with 1:16 remaining he hit the free throw for his 27th
point, which put Wake up by the final margin. With his 7 blocks,
Tim surpassed Georgetown's Alonzo Mourning to become the all-
time leader in blocked shots during a NCAA Tournament.

Wake's tournament win streak ended with an 83-63 loss to
powerhouse Kentucky, which had beat its first 3 tournament
opponents by 38, 24, and 31 points. The Wake team could not
match the depth of talent on the Kentucky Wildcat team. This
meant that Kentucky could focus attention on Tim. They held him
to 3 field goals in the first half. Kentucky's shooting was much more

accurate than Wake's. Tim came back in the second half and had 14 points and 16 rebounds for the game. He was the only player hitting for the Deacons.

Wake ended the 1995-96 season with 26 wins and 6 losses. They had tied the previous year's record. Tim was named for the second consecutive year the National Association of Basketball Coaches' defensive player of the year.

For the third straight year, Tim turned down the NBA draft, although he would probably have been the number one pick. By returning to college for his senior season, Tim passed up a chance at a three-year, $9 million contract. His family and friends gave him advice, but did not try to pressure him. Cheryl and Ricky now lived in Winston-Salem. Tim thought the decision to stay in college to be an easy one to make. He enjoyed college life, and there was still one more chance that he could play on a national champion college team.

Tim signed up for the first session of summer school in 1996 so that he could graduate on time the following spring. He spent the rest of the summer playing for the U.S. 22-and-under team, first against the American Olympic Dream Team, then in Puerto Rico against Canada. In that game, Tim had 16 points and 9 rebounds to lead 5 players in double figures.

Chapter Six

Entering the 1996-97 season, Tim Duncan was hungry to win another ACC championship. He also thought the Demon Deacons had a chance to win the NCAA championship.

The Wake team proved impressive. Ricky Peral was back at forward. There was a new 7' 1" freshman, Loren Woods, and the backcourt team of Braswell and Rutland had returned.

Tim was the only unanimous pick for the Associated Press pre-season All-America team. He also headed the list of pre-season candidates for the Naismith Award, given annually to the nation's top college basketball player. His dominance of the sport was also evident in another way—all but 5 of Wake's 1996-97 games were scheduled to be televised.

Wake Forest started the season ranked third in the nation, and easily beat Virginia Military Institute 92-63. Wake had similar luck against The Citadel, winning 86-52. Tim jammed, grabbed, and spun his way to 21 points and 12 rebounds. He hit 8 of 9 shots from the floor for the second half. The University of Richmond and Mississippi State faced the same fate. "Even when we executed," one Ole Miss player complained, "Tim blocked shots. There is nothing you can do about that. It's talent."

Tim positioned himself easily as team leader, saying frequently to teammates, "I'll handle that." Said Coach Odom, "When he talks, people listen. He's not given to a lot of babbling, and you won't see a lot of chest-bumping and fist-shaking. But the leadership is there in spirit and in truth. He doesn't say one thing and do another. There's no hypocrisy in what he does."

After Wake defeated Carolina 81-57, Tarheel Coach Dean Smith said, "Duncan is improved over last year. He's handling double-team tactics better, and he's passing better. But it's his presence on defense that makes them so hard to beat. They can afford to play you the way they want outside because they know he's back there to block shots and limit you to one shot."

Tim had become a legend in college basketball. Wofford College Coach Richard Johnson told his players before a game against Wake, "Let me tell you guys about who you're playing tomorrow. Someday your six-year-old kid will ask you for a Tim Duncan jersey for Christmas. This is your chance to play a future NBA Hall of Famer, your turn to face the greatest player any of you will ever meet."

In a 73-65 victory over Missouri, Wake clinched the game with an 18-2 run to open the second half. Tim did not have a single point during that stretch. It did not matter—he was still critical to Wake's win. "It seems like every time you turn around he's staring you in the face," said Tigers forward Derek Grimm. "I could have sworn there were four or five Tim Duncans out there." His 3 blocks against Missouri pushed him past Georgetown's Alonzo Mourning into second place on the NCAA's all-time blocked-shot list.

As often as not, Tim played the full 40 minutes of the game. In 10 ACC games, he had been on the bench for only 9 minutes. He had guided the Deacons to a 19-2 record, including a 4-0 mark on the road against Top 10 teams. By now Tim was taking 43 % of Wake's free throws—meaning he was being fouled consistently because he was a constant defensive target. He also led in turnovers, but that was because the ball came to him so often.

Wake finally got back to winning and defeated Georgia Tech at their last home game of the season. Tim's team retired his number, 21, and fans hoisted a replica of his jersey to the rafters of Wake's home court. The territorial governor of the Virgin Islands, the local congressman, and Tim's family were present. A shy Tim said to the crowd, "This is the first time in my life I've felt uncomfortable on a basketball court." His father, William, said, "The slogan I always gave Tim was 'Do your best and let it rest.'"

At the end of the regular season, Tim had 81 double doubles and 95 wins in 123 games over 4 years. He was named national college player of the year for 1996-97 season and was a two-time All-America first-team selection. He was only the tenth player in NCAA Division I history to score 2,000 points and grab 1,500 rebounds in his college career.

Wake was favored to win the ACC tournament for the third straight time. It was not to be, however. While Tim remained at the top of his game, the rest of the team had gone cold. Wake fell to Carolina, 86-73.

Tim was a unanimous choice for All-American, and for the second straight year he was named ACC player of the year. He was the number one all-time rebounder in ACC history and the number two scorer.

In the first round game of the NCAA tournament, Tim faced a gigantic center—Brad "Big Continent" Millard, who stood 7' 3", weighed 345 pounds, and wore size 22 sneakers. Millard's job was to "push" Tim around. It was exhausting work and he tired during the second half. Tim succeeded in keeping himself between Millard and the basket. He managed 22 points and 22 rebounds against Millard in Wake's 68-46 victory.

In the second round of the tournament against Stanford, Tim played against Brevin Knight, who he had roomed with the previous summer during the Pan-American Games. Said Knight, "I'm a neat person. I'm the type who folds up clothes and puts them away. Tim was the opposite. When he took off his clothes, they would wind up everywhere and anywhere." Responded Tim, "Brevin has a drawer fetish." The two players had frequent video game confrontations.

Their confrontation on the court did not go well for Tim. Stanford beat Wake, 72-66. Wake's shooters were cold and Stanford kept the ball from Tim in the second half. This game marked the end of Tim's college career.

Coach Odom was sorry to lose Tim. "Tim leaves us after four years of absolutely great performances—one monster game after another. I'm sad to see him go, but it's his time, and he's earned it. And as he walks out that door the last time, there will be no tears. Well, O.K. there will be tears."

Tim won all the major awards for college player of the year—the Naismith, the Sporting News, the Adolph Rupp, the U.S. Basketball Writers' Association, CBS Sports, The National Association of Basketball Coaches, and the John Wooden. These were prestigious honors and Tim was proud, but in many ways the highest honor he received, at least in his opinion, was earning his Bachelor's of Arts degree in psychology. He was now one of the few NBA prospects who had actually finished college.

Chapter Seven

In the NBA draft lottery, the teams with the worst record the year before get to choose first. Tim was the first choice of the San Antonio Spurs. They signed him to a three-year contract worth slightly more than $10 million.

Tim's signing set off a stampede to the Spur's box office. The fans hoped to see a major turnaround in the team's fortunes. Tim signed up for the NBA's summer camp in Utah, where he got his first taste of pro play. Tim was not awestruck at the prospect of playing in the pros. He had already played against many NBA players, such as Hakeem Olajuwon and Grant Hill, in college games or in international tournaments.

There was a risk that Tim would not turn out to be a great star. There had been other highly touted college players who failed in the NBA. The pressure was on to prove that he was not just a "flash-in-the-pan" player. He had ruled college basketball, but how would he do in the big league? There were many fans in San Antonio who eagerly—and nervously—awaited the answer.

In a way, Tim was starting over again in basketball. It was only 8 years since he had played his first organized game, but Tim had one advantage as he joined the last place Spurs. Their miserable record that year was because star big man David Robinson had missed most of the season with a back injury. Robinson was now well and ready for the 1997-98 season.

There was the question of how well the two big guys would get along. Would the 7' 1' David Robinson consider Tim a rival and try to undermine him? David was a nine-year veteran of the NBA who had once been voted the league's most valuable player and had played in the All-Star game 7 times. If David and Tim were unable to cooperate it would stop the team dead in its tracts.

Both players realized this. Soon after Tim was drafted, David invited him to his summer home in Aspen, Colorado. They quickly became friends, and it was not long before the duo, nicknamed the "Twin Towers," had figured out how to help each other in games. David became a teacher to Tim, working with him on his foul shooting and generally getting him "up" for games. Each had the ability to play either center or power forward, depending on which team they were up against. When one was guarding a tall player, the other could be at the basket to block a dunk. David also knew all the other teams' moves, and he told Tim what to look for.

Wearing the same "21" he had worn at Wake Forest, Tim began contributing to his new team at once. In a pre-season game, he had 20 points and 10 rebounds as the Spurs beat the Washington Wizards 96-76. In another pre-season game, he impressed star Charles Barkley of the Houston Rockets. "I have seen the future and he wears number 21." Rockets coach Rudy Tomjanovich added, "That play where he dribbles to his left and shoots it from high over his head—he's going to get that shot every time he wants it. People are going to have to do something to stop him from starting that move."

In the first regular game of the season, Tim had 15 points, 10 rebounds, 2 blocks, and 4 turnovers, as the Spurs beat the Denver Nuggets, 107-96.

It was not long before Tim was regularly scoring 20 points or more per game. Without David Robinson during the previous season, the Spurs had finished a lowly 20-62. The Spurs began the new season with 10 wins and 10 losses. Then they began to click and won 11 of 12. Tim and David were providing most of the offense, combining for an average of 42.1 points and 24.4 rebounds per game.

Unlike some other players, Tim did not like to do interviews, mug for the cameras, scream when he dunked, or wear strange jewelry. He did wear his practice shorts backward for luck. Some reporters thought he did not have a sense of humor, but that was because he kept his true self out of the media glare. Once he got his team to laugh by pretending to be a teammate who would get so mad at referees he would hop around. And, when Coach Popovich told him at the airport that rookies were supposed to grab the bags, Tim made such a big show of pretending to unload all the suitcases that his teammates laughed too hard to object when he never actually picked up their luggage.

Tim was named Rookie of the Month in November and December, and joined Robinson on the All-Star team. He was only the second rookie to ever make the All-Star team. David Robinson had been the first.

In February, when an inflamed right knee sidelined David, Tim found himself on his own. He responded by leading the team to 4 victories in the next 6 games. He was again selected as February's Rookie of the Month, and was already being called one of the top 3 players in the league.

David Robinson was impressed: "He's much further along than I was as a rookie. He has the baby hook, the spin moves, a consistent jump shot. It really is scary, given how young Tim is."

It was a close race for first place in the Midwest Division of the NBA. Then, in early April, the Utah Jazz beat the Spurs 98-88 to clinch the Midwest Division title. Fortunately, the Spurs' record of 47 wins and 22 defeats qualified them for a wild card berth in the playoffs.

In the first playoff game, Tim's bank shots, turnaround jumpers, between-the-legs ball handling, and running hook shots produced 32 points. This scoring and 10 rebounds helped the Spurs to a 102-96 victory over the Phoenix Suns. "When he gets in a zone there's nothing you can do to stop him," said one Suns player. "The only thing you can do is try to contain him."

The Suns did contain him in game 2 with a double-team defense. In the 108-101 loss, Tim was held to 16 points, 10 rebounds, and 4 blocked shots. That was good enough for most players, but it was low for him.

Tim came back in the next 2 games, and the Spurs won the series 3-1. In the final game, Tim had 22 points and 14 rebounds in San Antonio's 100-88 victory. This time he figured out how to split the double-team or find the open man. His playing reminded many in the crowd of another great rookie from over a decade before—Michael Jordan.

The Spurs advanced to the Western Conference Semifinals, but the Utah Jazz proved to be much more formidable than the Suns. The Jazz beat the Spurs in the first game 83-82. Tim dominated offensively and defensively, outscoring the entire Jazz team 17-15 in the fourth quarter, but he missed a game-winning jump shot. Utah won the second game, 109-106 in overtime. The Spurs finally won one from the Jazz 86-84 in game 3 although Tim was held to 10 points and 10 rebounds. In the fourth game, the Jazz won 82-73. Tim had 22 points. In the fifth game, the Jazz won the best-of-seven series, 87-77.

The Spurs' season was over, but it had been a success. They had enjoyed the greatest turnaround in league history, from a 20-62 record in 1996-97, to 56-26 in 1997-98. Tim and David had averaged more than 20 points each per game.

Tim had averaged 21.1 points, 11.9 rebounds, and 2.5 blocks his first year. He was the first rookie since Larry Bird in 1980 to make the All-NBA first team. He won Rookie of the Year and finished fifth in the balloting for league MVP.

Tim Duncan had quieted any doubts about his ability to play in the pros. His next goal was to achieve what his college team had never been able to accomplish. Tim wanted the San Antonio Spurs to become the NBA Champions.

Chapter Eight

Tim Duncan makes millions of dollars a year. He lives with his fianceè, Amy Sherrill, a former Wake Forest cheerleader, and 2 Labrador retrievers named Shadoe and Zen, in a 4,500-square-foot house on the edge of San Antonio. It is a big house with a swimming pool, but it is not a mansion. His prize possessions are a large knife collection and a huge collection of video games.

Tim is a casual dresser who prefers jeans and a T-shirt. He is careful with his money. He has set up his own website (SlamDuncan.com) to keep in touch with his fans.

When he is not playing, he might be practicing or working out. He does not care much for nightclubs. He prefers a quiet meal at home and watching TV—especially professional wrestling. Tim also donates his time and money to charity. He works with the Spurs Foundation, the United Way, and the Children's Bereavement Center, an organization that helps young people who have lost a parent. Tim also works to bring business opportunities and new sporting facilities to his home island of St. Croix.

The 1998-99 season was delayed because of a wage dispute. During the extended break, Tim appeared in a humorous soft drink commercial with Detroit Pistons star Grant Hill. The ad showed them mowing grass and delivering newspapers, temporary jobs until the season got on a roll.

Tim also wrote a magazine article explaining himself to the sportswriters and fans that thought he was aloof and unfriendly. He called it "What Lurks Behind That Smirk: The Psychoanalysis of Tim Duncan."

In the article, Tim wrote that he sometimes seems standoffish because he's a shy, quiet person who is constantly thinking and analyzing things. He likes to figure out what makes people act the way they do, and he likes to get others to relax. Once, when the Spurs were in a close game, his friend and teammate Avery Johnson "missed two or three lay-ups in a row and was starting to stress out. I just came over and asked him something out of the blue—something like, 'What kind of music do you like to listen to?' He just looked at me real funny, like 'What the heck are you talking about? Why isn't your mind on the game?' Then he looked at me, and I think he understood what I was saying. 'It's not a big deal. It happened. It's gone. We can't change it now. Think about something else.'"

To his friends Tim is funny and charming. Says Antonio Daniels, "He busts into my room on road trips, and if there's a basketball game on, he makes me turn to wrestling. We're in each other's rooms hours a day, watching TV and laughing."

On the court, Tim tries not to show his emotions. "Basketball is like a chess game, you cannot reveal all that you are thinking or you will be at a sizable disadvantage to your opponent."

Tim does not make for good newspaper stories because he is so dependable. He is on time for practice. He does not complain if someone else has the ball. He does not argue with referees, hang on the rim after a dunk, or brag to the reporters. When he gets angry, only the players know it. "I see him sitting on the bench, making faces," Spurs guard Mario Elie says. "I know when he's mad."

The 1998-99 season did not start until February and was shortened from 82 to 50 games. The Spurs started out slowly, winning only 6 of their first 14 games. Then Tim and the team began to click, winning one game after another. When they beat the Sacramento Kings 101-83, Tim scored 19 points and delighted the fans with his dunks. That week he was chosen for the U.S. Olympic team.

Tim was displaying a newfound determination and intensity. He and Robinson would regularly score 35 or 40 points and block or alter dozens of shots. Most of the opposition fell to their hot shooting and heads-up play, including the best in the league—the Rockets, the Trailblazers, the Jazz, and the Lakers. Tim could beat his opponents with anything and everything—left-handed push shots, corner jumpers, right-handed hooks, drop-steps, pivot foots, and free throws. He did not need the glamorous three-pointers and the slam dunks. He was virtually impossible to stop one-on-one.

By April the Spurs were 34-13. At one point in an 84-78 victory over the Jazz, Tim grabbed a rebound from Jazz star Karl Malone and jammed it into the basket. The huge home crowd, the largest of the season, exploded in chants of "M-V-P, M-V-P!"

Tim made the cover of *Sports Illustrated*, but when the team offered him extra copies, he declined. He had already bought one, read it, and thrown it away. The article had referred to his "stone" face and lack of emotion, his total disregard for the media, and his lack of personality. Tim laughed it off—they did not know him.

The Spurs easily won the Midwest Division crown. They had the same record as the Jazz, 37-13, which tied them for the best in the NBA, but they had won their season series against the Jazz, 2-1. And they had done it without showy dunks, high elbows, and trash talking. The Spurs were a steady, disciplined basketball team that quietly dominated their opposition.

In the first round of the playoffs, they rolled over the Minnesota Timberwolves 3 games to one. Tim was voted to the NBA All-Defense team.

With Tim's dad watching from the stands, the Spurs swept the Los Angeles Lakers in 4 games to win the Western Conference semifinals. In the third game, Tim had a career playoff high of 37 points, including 19 free throws. Tim dunked and hit short jumpers. Unlike Shaquille O'Neal, the Lakers' big man, he hit his foul shots.

It was the same story in the conference championship against the Portland Trailblazers. The Spurs won in 4 straight games, including one by 44 points. Tim was chosen for the All-NBA first team. He lost out for MVP to Karl Malone.

The Spurs were in the NBA championship series against the New York Knicks, who would be playing without their star, Patrick Ewing, who was injured. One hundred and seventy-five of Tim's friends flew to San Antonio for the first game. They were in the stands as Tim made 33 points and 16 rebounds to lead the Spurs to an 89-77 win over the Knicks. Tim did it all—20-foot jumpers from beyond the free throw line, bank shots from the wings, lay ups with each hand, foul shots, and rebound tip-ins.

The Spurs won the second game, 80-67, but the Knicks won the third, 89-81. It was the first time the Spurs had lost in 41 days. Tim scored 20 points, although the triple-teaming slowed him down. The Spurs came back to win the fourth game, 96-69. Tim had 28 points, and all the Spurs starters were in the double figures.

And then came the fifth and last game—the duel with an

inspired Latrell Sprewell that came down to one missed shot.

Tim had averaged 23.2 points and 11.5 rebounds in the first 3 playoff series and 27.4 points, 14 rebounds, and 2.2 blocks in the series against New York.

When the Spurs returned to San Antonio they were greeted by thousands of fans at the airport. Some fans had been waiting for 2 hours in the rain. Avery Johnson held the championship trophy aloft for all to see. The post-game celebration lasted for hours with thousands of fans filling the downtown streets.

During the summer of 1999, Tim joined the U.S. national basketball team in a series to prepare for the 2000 Summer Olympic Games in Sydney, Australia. On September 7, 1999, the Spurs visited the White House, where President Clinton stated he was a basketball fanatic. Basketball was like politics, he said: "You get ahead, you get behind. Normally, you don't know whether you are going to win until it's right before the end of the game."

The president confided to the team that he hoped he could learn a lesson from Tim: He wanted to develop his "killer look" for budget negotiations that fall.

The Spurs told the president they wanted to keep improving. Their goal was to contend in the 2000 championships.

With Tim Duncan leading the way, it seemed a reasonable wish.

Glossary

Assist: A pass to a teammate that leads directly to a goal.

Bank shot: Bouncing the ball off the backboard at an angle so it drops into the basket.

Center: Usually the tallest member of the team, who often plays with his back to the basket on offense and tries to set up shots and block the other team's shots.

Crossover dribble: Dribbling the ball back and forth from one hand to the other.

Double-team: Two defensive players guarding one offensive player. A dangerous move, because it leaves one offensive player unguarded.

Elbowing: Excessive swinging of the elbows near another player. A foul can be called if contact is made.

Fake: Throwing a defender off balance with a deceptive move that allows an offensive player to shoot or receive a pass.

Field goal: A successful two- or three-point shot taken from anywhere on the court during play.

Field goal percentage: Calculated by dividing the field goals made by field goals attempted and multiplying by one hundred.

Forwards: The major playmakers on a team who are usually smaller than the center and bigger than the guards.

Foul: Illegal contact with an opponent. Penalty is either a free throw or a change in possession.

Foul shot: See "free throw".

Free throw: Unopposed shot for the basket from the free throw line after a player is fouled. Worth one point.

Free throw lane (or "free throw key"): Rectangular area under the basket between the free throw line and the end line. Offensive players cannot stay in this area more than three seconds while teammates have possession of the ball in the frontcourt.

Free throw percentage: Calculated by dividing free throws made by free throws attempted and multiplying by one hundred.

Guards: Smaller players who help set up plays and pass to teammates closer to the basket.

Jump shot: A field goal attempt taken by a player with one hand while jumping.

Layup: A one-hand shot made after driving close to the basket, leaping up, and banking the ball from the backboard into the basket.

MVP (Most Valuable Player): Award to the player who contributed most in the regular season or in the finals.

NBA (National Basketball Association): The major professional basketball league.

NCAA (National Collegiate Athletic Association): A standard-setting sports association of over a thousand colleges and universities in the U.S.

NCAA Tournament: Annual competition between 64 college teams with the best records to crown a national champion

Overtime: Extra period or periods played after a regulation game ends in a tie.

Rebound: Recovering the ball after a failed shot.

Salary cap: Annual limit that a single team may pay its players.

Three-point shot: A field goal shot at least 22 feet from the basket.

Time-out: Period when play is temporarily suspended by an official, or at the request of a team to discuss strategy or see to an injured player.

Triple double: Scoring double-digits in three categories during one game—usually points, assists, and rebounds, but might also include blocks.

Turnover: The offense losing possession by passing the ball out of bounds or committing a floor violation.

Zone defense: Defense used in college ball where each defender is responsible for guarding an area of the court.

Statistics

College Stats	FG%	RPG	PPG
1993-94	54.5	9.6	9.8
1994-95	59.1	12.5	16.8
1995-96	55.5	12.3	19.1
1996-97	60.8	14.7	20.8

College Achievements

First-Team All-ACC 1995-97
NABC National Defensive Player of the Year 1995-97
First-Team All-American 1996-97
ACC Player of the Year 1996-97
Naismith Award 1997
Wooden Award 1997
Associated Press Player of the Year 1997

Pro Stats	FG%	RPG	PPG
1997-98	54.9	11.9	21.1
1998-99	49.5	11.4	21.7

Pro Achievements

NBA Rookie of the Year 1998
NBA All-Star 1998
First-Team All-NBA 1998-99
NBA All-Defensive First Team 1999
NBA Finals MVP 1999
NBA Champion 1999

Bibliography

"Demon Deacon," Tim Crothers, *Sports Illustrated*, February 17, 1997.

"Duncan in(Tim)idates Lakers," Cammy Clark, *Orange County Register*, May 23, 1999.

"Duncan Pushed Spurs to the Top," The Associated Press, *Greensboro News & Record*, June 26, 1999.

"Duncan's Day," by Mark Starr and Nadine Joseph, *Newsweek*, May 17, 1999.

"Duncan, the VH1 of Superstars," Chris Broussard, *N.B.A. Finals*, June 16, 1999.

"Easy Does It," Richard Hoffer, *Sports Illustrated*, May 31, 1999.

"Getting Schooled," David Higdon, *Boys' Life*, January, 1998.

"Grant's Tomb," Jackie MacMullan, *Sports Illustrated*, February 9, 1998.

"Kids Ask," Ellen Cosgrove and Marlene Rooney, *Sports Illustrated for Kids*, December, 1998.

"Knicks Lack Answers for Tim Duncan," Mark Whicker, *Orange County Register*, June 17, 1999.

"Life Hasn't Always Been a Breeze for Duncan," Ed Hardin, *Greensboro News and Record*, March 6, 1997.

"Mission Accomplished," David Robinson and Phil Taylor, *Sports Illustrated*, July 7, 1999.

"Mr. Robinson Shares His Neighborhood," Douglas S. Looney, *Christian Science Monitor*, June 25, 1999.

"A Mystery in Prime Time," Jeff Ryan, *Sporting News*, June 7, 1999.

"The NBA Puts Tim Duncan On Center Stage," Ed Hardin, *Greensboro News and Record*, June 25, 1997.

"No Longer Battle of Equals As Camby Faces Duncan," Steve Popper, *N.B.A. Finals*, June 14, 1999.

"Out of Reach?" John Delong, *Winston-Salem Journal*, June 14, 1999.

"Rear Admiral," Phil Taylor, *Sports Illustrated*, April 12, 1999.

"Rested Duncan Set to Dominate for National Team," L. C. Johnson, *Orlando Sentinel*, July 7, 1999.

"Spur of the Moment," Jackie MacMullan, *Sports Illustrated*, May 4, 1998.

"Spurs' Tim Duncan May be Quiet, But There is Nothing Silent About His Play," Sam Smith, *Chicago Tribune*, March 15, 1998.

"Spurs' Tim Duncan Shows Why He's Rookie of the Year," David Moore, *Dallas Morning News*, April 28, 1998.

"Statitudes," Jack McCallum and Richard O'Brien, *Sports Illustrated*, April 13, 1998.

"Texas' Nice Guys Just May Finish First," Scott Baldauf, *Christian Science Monitor*, June 16, 1999.

"Tim Duncan Has More Personality Than He'll Let Us See," Jesse Barkin, *San Jose Mercury News*, June 18, 1999.

"Two For the Show," Phil Taylor, *Sports Illustrated*, November 24, 1997.

"What Lurks Behind That Smirk: The Psychoanalysis of Tim Duncan," Tim Duncan, *Sport Magazine*, March, 1999.

Index